Elves, Gods, and Spirits

Children's Norse Folktales

BABY PROFESSOR

EDUCATION KIDS

Speedy Publishing LLC
40 E. Main St. #1156
Newark, DE 19711
www.speedypublishing.com
Copyright 2016

The Norse believed in supernatural beings. They even had feasts and other ways to celebrate the mythical creatures.

Let's get to know
some of these
magical creatures.

ELVES

An elf is considered as a kind of demigod-like being. They are luminous and more beautiful than the sun. It is not clear as to how to differentiate elves from gods and dwarves. The people did not set a clear distinction for them.

Elves' relationship with humans is ambivalent. Elves can cause human sickness. But they also have the power to heal them if people are willing to offer sacrifices for them.

Elves and humans
can interbreed and
bear half-human
children who have a
human appearance
but possess
magical powers
and extra-ordinary
intuitiveness.

Some people believed that humans could becomes elves after they die and so there is somehow an overlap of the worship of ancestors and the worship of elves.

GODS

There are many
Norse gods and
goddesses. These
are much like
the Greek gods
and goddesses.

The Norse gods are divided into two major groups, the Vanir and Aesir, aside from the giants who ruled the world before them.

The Vanir gods are
the older pantheon,
or group of gods.
The Aesir, who are
the newcomers,
overcame the Vanir.

Odin is the chief
of all the gods. He
is the god of war
and death, wisdom
and poetry. He can
make the dead
speak and question
the wisest among
them. He observes
all that is happening
in the nine worlds.

The most famous
of the Norse gods
is Thor. He is the
son of Odin and
the earth goddess
Jord. Thor is the
god of thunder.

Loki is the god
of thieves and is
a giant in Norse
mythology. He
is the adopted
brother of Odin.

SPIRITS

Land Spirits are the localized animating spirits of the land. They wield a lot of influence on the well-being of the land and all who depend on it.

They can curse or
bless the people
who live or travel
within their land.
They protect their
native lands and
will not tolerate
mistreatment or
dishonor of them.

The people in earlier times took great care to maintain favor with the land spirits. They had it in their law that those who arrive in the country by ship should remove the dragon heads from the boats as they see the land so they will not frighten the land spirits when they come close to shore.

The belief on the
land spirits continues
today with the
pagan Aasatru
Association as
the most obvious
believers. They have
set restrictions
on some farms
and natural areas,
trying to keep
certain rocks and
holy places from
being disturbed
or even mowed.

Visit

BABY PROFESSOR
EDUCATION KIDS

www.BabyProfessorBooks.com

to download Free Baby Professor eBooks and view
our catalog of new and exciting Children's Books